NOW YOU SEE ME

Complete Poetry Book

Jason Refsnider

Farrah Hodgson
Daughter of the King Publishing

Now You See Me : Complete Poetry Book
Copyright © 2019 by Jason Refsnider.

All rights reserved. Printed in the United States of America. No part of this book may be used or reproduced in any manner whatsoever without written permission except in the case of brief quotations em- bodied in critical articles or reviews.

Published By : Daughter of the King Publishing

ISBN: 978-0-578-22750-4

First Edition: December 2019

10 9 8 7 6 5 4 3 2 1

TABLE OF CONTENTS

About the Author	Jason Refsnider
Introduction	Jason Refsnider
Chapter 1	Opening Remarks
Chapter 2	The Blame Game
Chapter 3	Reflections
Chapter 4	Keynote
Chapter 5	Auditions
Chapter 6	Out of Tune
Chapter 7	In Tune
Chapter 8	The Turning Point
Chapter 9	Debut
Chapter 10	Release Date
Chapter 11	Nominated

About the Author

Jason Refsnider, otherwise known as *"J Speaks"*, was born in Wilmington, Delaware where he lived for three months, but currently resides in Altamonte Springs, Florida. While he was growing, he lived in four different States because his father was always looking for better employment opportunities.

In 2014, he went through a major transition during his college years when father decided to divorce his mother. . They both attended the same church and he didn't realize how much this would impact him at the church he was attending at the time. It was difficult to forgive his father, but it was an important step he needed to make.

From 2016 until 2017 he invested a lot of his time with his father. After reconciling with his father, Jason decided to do what's best for his future. Of course, things don't always go as planned. This is why you call major decisions a "leap of faith". That said, Florida drew his attention because of a close bond with a family friend. On August 28, 2017, all employees were fired from the company he was working for, and that's when Jason decided to make a huge move. Fast forward to 42 days later, he packed up and headed south. There has been no looking back since. The first year was difficult because he had to trust in God and himself more than ever before. There was no running back to his mom for a hug or a conversation in the kitchen. No hanging out with his sister anymore on a weekly basis.

It was hard, but character and confidence would become the foundation that he built his life around.
Since the transition, he's accomplished full independence for himself, developing great friendships and mentors along the way, and now he's becoming an Author. In Maryland, he finished third at a poetry slam, released his own rap single and spoken word single. He does not believe in coincidence, because he's been on a faith journey.
All the decisions now fall on his shoulders, but that doesn't scare him, it drives him to create a better future for himself. So, taking chances is becoming a second nature process. Has it been easy? No. Has he faced more challenges here? Absolutely. But all in all, the character, integrity, and strength he's gained has been worth every setback. It feels good to know he holds the keys to unlocking his imagination. Here's a quote he lives by now. **"If you are not willing to risk the unusual, you will have to settle for the ordinary."**

Contact information:
Email: Jason.refsnider@yahoo.com
Facebook: https://www.facebook.com/jrefsnider1990
Phone: 321-888-0600

INTRODUCTION

This is dedicated to my Mom and Momma Bear for encouraging me to start publishing my work, and to my sister for being the sibling who is "thick as thieves".

The goal of this book is for readers to investigate deep within themselves, so God can show them what they are meant to manifest in this world. I hope you not only see the real version of me, but you also discover the real you. Whatever "itch" burns inside your soul, tap into that reality and see where it takes you.

I'm grateful for every win and loss I've experienced. It's given me the right tools on how to handle every circumstance that comes my way. So, hop on board and let's go down a road to figure out the breath that's supposed to be breathing out of your lungs.

Chapter 1: Opening Remarks

What do you see?

What do you see?
A 14-year-old inner critic
Scoffing at his intentions
Of becoming a person who can
Reach for stars beyond his dreams
An alpha type of man who fully attaches his soul toward Faith
Where he can utilize the tools in his hands
And make all things Impossible become possible
What do you see?
A voice of fear which stirs
Up theories parading around his mind
In hopes that he never discovers what
Power can be unlocked inside
Once he opens the door, he'll realize through real eyes
There's nothing on earth that can slow him down
From spreading a light that glows across the skies
What do you see?
Tell me, what do you see?
A constant trailer of a family tree
Which is never coming back
What do you see?
Running away from the idea of becoming great
Or recognizing that all those wins and losses
Were just setting up for this date with destiny today
What do you see?
A person of high value or low value
A person who takes courage in the face of fear
A person who stands even if nobody else stands with him
What do you see?
The wondering soul
That already knows what he should focus on
He keeps on hearing the screams day after day
"Set me free, oh J remember how to Speak."
Whatever you see
I want to change the way I see you and the way you see me

Family Album: Part 1

Come kids, gather around the mistletoe
Let us collect memories of these precious moments
Don't forget to spend time reading about the baby who provided
The reasons for this joyous season
Ahh, what a great story. Now let me grab my video camera
We are going to take turns unwrapping each present
Now I must be present so I can hang these reactions
On portraits for your kids and our grandkids
The recording is finished, everyone is now in bed
Now to document all these files
Hold up? Where did the film go?

Family Album: Part 2

I swear I just had the pictures
Where are they now?
Honey! Kids! Can you help me find the film?
Crickets. Crickets. Crickets
No response! That's strange
What is going on?
Wait a minute, I deleted them for good
Now those photos are just a distant memory
Never to be seen
Where did I go wrong?
I had this pure intention but now it's a lost message
I'm confined to this living room of silence
Holiday seasons are going to be hard for them
Because I split up the family album.

Homeschooled

10 years of sitting behind a desk
The dust of boredom started piling up after age 10
I remember breathing a fresh breath
Of air when the decision was made
To grab a backpack and be outside with other
People my age throughout
An entire semester.

Transitions

The ship is sailing again
Come let's go now!
But I just got the hang of everything!
Well that's how it goes sometimes
Sigh. Okay.

Memory Lane

Hey Josh, you remember
When Me, you, Chris, and Steven
Pranked our Youth Counsellor
With Icy Hot?
Oh yeah, we smothered his shirts
With so much Icy hot
The look on his face was Priceless
He looked like the Hulk
When he got angry
Me: I'm standing there awkwardly
I have no idea what they're laughing about
It would have been great being
In that moment. Oh well, such is life
Memory lanes come in bits and Pieces for me.

Partner in Crime

Accusations. Assumptions. Fights. Yelling
This chaos spreading around the house
Thank God for my partner in crime
This sibling power has a Batman and Robin
Tomboy and Boy
No matter what happened behind closed doors
We still had each other's back
To keep our posture straight.

Full House

Home is where the heart is
Well my heart is still wondering
Around in search of a full house
The kind of house
That looks to remain full
Without excuses being made
The kind of house
From the widowed man Danny
His brother in law Jesse
And their best friend Joey
Working as one unit
To raise Danny's three little girls
Now that's what I call
Keeping a house full.

Josiah

What's going on Josiah?
I see you've come from
A bloodline of people
Who are inherently evil
Wish you could live in the
Same house as me so I could
Emulate your daily habits
But all I have is your story
And that's not good enough.

You wouldn't

You would never know
The constant disconnection I felt
Because in the sunshine
It almost didn't seem real
I was always a kid afraid
To ask for help.

Will I ever

Will I ever muster up
The courage to finally
Speak what's on my mind.
I look at the dictionary of
Definitions I've defined
As my truths
However, I refuse
To share what's
Going on with me
I would like to step outside
This front door and feel
Normal around my fears
But again, I should keep
The tape on because I have
Nothing of interests to say.

Grace

Go find somewhere else
Reconsider what you created
Are you hearing me right now?
Come on, there's nothing of value here
Exit the room of my life on your right

Mercy

Maybe instead of giving me another chance
Examine a heart who goes up and down with commitment
Read the book of life with a family tree without flaws
Can't you see I can't even believe enough in myself
You'll understand eventually and that's when you'll leave

Peace

Puzzles fall right on the floor
Each time I'm trying to piece the puzzle together
Around the corner I'll hear an ocean of disturbance
Cannot keep myself focused on the moment at hand
I enter into the panic room and that's when the pieces go missing.

Chapter 2: The Blame Game

Will I ever see?

I want black and white
For some reason I'm scared to
Show my true colors

Fourteen

There I was sitting on a chair looking at a blank word document
Stuck in the office room downstairs
The paper assignment was due in a few hours
Knowing me though, I was browsing Myspace
While leaving the document sitting by itself
The closer I got to the deadline, the more my anxiety built up
Leading up to this situation
I was having a conversation with my creative consultant, Jay
He wanted to participate but those same little errors kept showing up in the memory file cabinet Every time he started typing out his thoughts
So many different voices were convincing me to not bother with "giving your best"
"Even in your best", I kept remembering the Father-figure
Declaring, with conviction in his tone of voice that
"You write like a third grader"
Why should I even bother? I said
Doesn't matter what happens, I'm going to hear the same lecture
With that said, there was enough sense of pride
To complete the assignment to move on toward better things
"Yes! The paper is completed, here goes nothing", I said
Printed out the final draft then yelled from the top of my lungs, "I'm finished."
This was only the beginning of what became a death sentence to my creative beliefs
The words he spoke would spread like a disease
In the inner being of my soul
If you ever caught me in conversations as a younger version
I would usually wonder off into another point of interests
And even though I was extroverted, there was a timid spirit running the show
All I ever heard was, "this writing process you put together is Kindergarten Work"
"Those paragraphs is 3rd grade level material"
This criticism hit me harder than someone leaving me behind
After this night, I wrestled with creating again
Even though deep down a voice was begging to come out of the closet
But I said please stop it before I find myself
In another relationship with disappointment
Those fragments are just a part of me

There's no way I can actually figure out how to really speak
My handwriting isn't the most eligible and that 3rd Grader mentality
Eats me alive
Spreading itself like a bad breakup

Tears of A Tiger

Reading was never my thing
But then Andy came around
His story kept me intrigued
His demons were hard to digest
It drove him straight to a state
Of mind he would never
Come back from again.

Bria

Hey Bria, I hope all is well
At 16 our fling felt so real
I know you didn't have it all together with God
But neither did I and that's what caught my eyes
You were quiet around the other kids
All those other girls dressed in their skirts
Didn't stop you from expressing
How you felt about being in the church
And that's what caught my attention
You spoke your mind while respecting
The leadership's convictions
Once we started talking
I didn't want our connection to end
I remember the last hug we exchanged
It was two people in search of meaning
And for one moment, that exchange
Kept us believing that maybe
Someday, love would become
Attractive to us.
If only I had a cell phone that was actually mine
Guess I will never know
But at least I got to understand
The importance of looking beyond
The outside of a woman's appearance
Thank you for that experience
I'm still wrestling with being secured
Despite the hurt, I'll cherish those conversations forever.

Blame it on the rain

Raindrops keep falling on my head
I said raindrops keep falling on my head
The storm has creased the pavement walls
Of my altered universe
I had this expectation all planned out
Step by step. There was nothing holding me back
The only thing left was to keep driving on the same route
Wait. Pause. Not this again
"Why me? Why me?", I asked
It just seems that going two steps forward and 5 steps backwards
Always has the final laugh
Put on Joker's mask cause I'm tired
The rain never stops falling on my side
I would like to catch a break
Maybe even get a little bit of sunshine
Well it's time to go back into my cocoon
Don't let anybody in for a couple of weeks
Once I'm done throwing my pity party
The rain won again
I'll slowly come back and find earth again.

The Past

I only look back
Because I've been programmed that way.

Good Things

At this point, I'm used to good things
Running away into the Shadows.

Attachment

The string reels
In many different interests
Some Interests begin at 90%
While other interests start at 10%
No matter where it starts
The chords begin painting the chorus
It harmonizes into
Something that's as sweet as a good night kiss
My brain gets excited with meeting new faces
I am preoccupied with
An expectation that
Our attachment will
Be forever connected
Until the ship moves on
Then another transition
Smacks me like a Sweet Chin Music in the face
Man, this cycle never seems to stop.

Gone Forever

Maybe if I was gone forever
It would give me
A sense of relief
Go find a bridge
And just say goodbye
I haven't seen a lot of reasons
To be alive
Yeah God is good
But what's the point
Of that statement
When you don't
See much good
From your own two eyes
The goodbye would be quick and easy
No one would actually care
That old man's voice
Has a strong hold on me.

Another Round

I'm sitting in the corner ring, hands down
Asking for a longer break

But my rounds never
Have any breaks
The exhaustion is wearing me down
I just want to fly away.

Mirrors

Mirror, mirror on the wall
When I look into my eyes
I'm trying to register the belief
That I am really a valuable prize
Something that doesn't have a price tag
For a retail customer to grab and buy
To be honest, I've attached myself to the mistakes I've made
It's had a good wireless connection
Where I'm hearing every single objection
I want to believe in this vision
But right now the mirror is making a strong case
That my ideas should focus itself on playing life safe
That no matter what endeavor I attempt
The results will always be the same as before
The voices ask, "what's the point of putting stock in a investment without return"
That I've had to learn certain lessons at a later stage than everybody else
Shouldn't I have picked up the hints a lot sooner?
Man, I'm hard on myself
I can't even snap my own fingers
Must be one of those outcasts who probably will never understand me
And even if I try to be understood it'll receive a casted stone
This comfort zone will remain my habitat
Okay Mirror on the wall, I'm just going to keep stalling on what I want out of myself
Go pack up those lines
Accept the facts
You are too late
The audition has already ended for you
Just move on with the crumbs you've been given
Yes, mirror on the wall, I'll continue living just below the potential inside of me
I look forward to the next morning with you
When these same old conversations will be silenced by your perspectives.

Chapter 3: Reflections

Dear Jay: Part 1

Dear Jay,
If I could take a time machine, I would go back to age six
Sit you down in the living room
Let you know that you'll take a lot of hits
I would tell you that life is going to be hard
When you have questions, go talk to God
When you feel like quitting, go talk to God
When you feel betrayed, go talk to God
Whatever setbacks you have, talk to God
I think you understand what I'm saying
Because He's the only that'll listen even if you believe He isn't
Yes, mom and dad are no longer together, they decided to break the vows
Hop on a different route
But it was never your fault
You've watched all those pictures closed shut
And I know it can feel worse than death, especially when both are still alive
And there's no opportunity of scrolling on your phone to look back at memories
You could look at with appreciation of the good times
And I understand you probably feel all the success falls on your shoulders
And to be honest I'm amazed you've made it this far
Six years walking on both feet
Without any warm hugs to comfort you on a daily basis
No one saying in the same room, "I love you"
No one saying, "Hey let's go out for a night together"
No affections waiting for you to come home
And remind you
That they've missed you
And I know the roots will never be the same now
However, the only process you control is the now
I'm also sorry you have to hear this
But you'll witness good people who'll love you then end up pushing your
Heart of gold into a place of confusion because they're scared of committing
Although their albums never had any of there family roles missing
It'll leave you in a pit where you start to think it's wasted effort
Toss and turn with the presence of fear eating up your insides
You won't project every U-turn coming
But just understand this process will put the pieces back together
I know it's hard at times finding the right moment to shine
And that's just fine
You might feel like a victim

But remember to never allow bitterness to block the power of forgiveness
And I know you find yourself living as the outcast sometimes
Where people seem to leave your circle
And have you questioning if you'll ever see clarity from the past
At this stage, you need to search
For the lines of hope
Walk through the battlefield
Take on the burdens of loneliness
Take on the pain for a little bit longer
One day you'll find yourself inspiring others
To expose their hurts
You'll come through the fire
For now, just keep going higher
Well my work for today is done.
Until next time Jay.

Two Face

On the right cheek of my face is purity
On the left cheek of my face is scarcity
The kind of scarcity
Where I'm constantly reminded
About what I didn't fulfill by a specific deadline
It's like a reminder on my phone
Never leaves you alone
Red notifications keep notifying me
I want greatness, but it's difficult to even see
Especially when you've gotten used to looking
At the shape of those imperfections.

Peter Pan

There is a Peter Pan inside of me
Many children were just like me
Then I grew up
The shadow didn't leave me
But I decided to lock up his imagination for good
Toss aside those possibilities
And exchanged my possible realities
For more reasonable expectations.

The Mask

Another morning has arrived
Now let's go into my closet
Oh yes
There is the green mask
I'm wearing this version again
All these impressions of who I'm not
Will make me look fly in the end
My life expresses Jim Carrey's
Type of Comedies
Gotta laugh.
If I make the transfer
Into a role of original acting
That might not workout
Well for me
So, cheers to wearing the mask
Thank God I can hide myself.

Held On

I've held on to thoughts
I've always wanted to share
The problem is, I have connected my soul to heartbreak
Even if I separate heart and break
There is a voice telling me
Keep those two connected
A heart of gold can't
Save you from the moment you break
Hold on for safety reasons.

Loaded Up

Am I the only one who's loading up a gun
Full of Fear and Anxiety
I complain when the bullets
Keep shooting right at me
Tell my friends one day I'll
Eventually move on from these memories
But honesty, I much rather keep loading
Up the same files that's destroying me
It's sad to see
But it's the only eyes I see in front of me.

The Little Guy

I have always seen
Myself as the little guy
Who appears out of
Touch with those around me
Maybe that's the reason
Why I attach myself
To crowds who struggle
Finding a place to be heard.

If Only

If only I could have a do over
Then maybe I would give
Myself another chance at love.

Fly Eagles Fly

I would like to fly,
But my eyes are
Fixated on the
Clipped wings.

Decisions

Being unsure of yourself
Being indecisive with yourself
Being confused about yourself
Is still a decision in itself.

The English Language

The period goes
Over here.
The comma
Goes in this section
The, their and there
Need another
Explanation.
That 14-year old kid
Still hasn't gone away.

People Pleaser

Yes! Yes! Yes!
I'm the "yes man"
Who is afraid to miss out
But even when I show up
I'm not really present.

Discomfort

This broken left hand
Is not prepared to restore
His spoken word yet.

Chapter 4:   Keynote

Keynote

How do you find a theme for someone who can't find the keys to his Identity crisis?
He's opened different presentations
And nothing has worked out correctly
Trying to learn
Different concepts
Different skills
But nothing has stuck
The keynote in this opening
Chapter is lack of hope for
A bright future.

Rhymes

A to B
C to D
D to S
M to A.
Hold on, where is the order I had envisioned in my head?
Why can't I just follow the simple protocol?

Heard

I've sat in circles
Where I might get a word in
But the melodies
Didn't come together.

Songs of myself

This is A sharp
This is B flat
This is C minus
So many octaves
Which make up a song
I'm having trouble
Finding the rhythm.

Safe Sounds

I like the safe sounds
The clothes folded
The bed made
The scent of chicken
Traveling into my
Game room downstairs.
My name called, two syllables
That echoes as loud as a volcano eruption
The dinner is primed and ready
I liked the safe sounds because it's
A safe house for inner peace.

Fear

Find myself at the court once again
Every time I take a seat, you've got objections ready
A loud standing ovation of torment cheers you on
Reminding me to speak up for myself.

Doubt

Danced around speaking up for myself
Offered a point of view but I declined
Unfazed appearance was on full display
But deep down I knew my mind had something to say
The problem was that my convictions were controlled by an indecisive soul.

Insecure

I stands for "I can't handle your eye contact for a long period of time"
N stands for "Now I'm doing this to protect myself from becoming myself"
S stands for "Settle down into a place of security, those destinies are over"
E stands for "Every January 1st I proclaim change, but never follow through"
C stands for "Commitment is an impossible mountain to climb"
R stands for "Run far, far, far away from the beauty of falling in love"
E stands for "Ego putting up a wall against following after my true passions".

Almost

I almost gave up
I said "Almost"
I hope almost
Never disappears
When the going gets tough.

I don't

I don't have trust issues
I have healing issues.

Trust

The only way
I can resolve trust problems
Is by giving my trust away.

I Can Only

I can only Imagine
The Future
But I can't
Imagine how
The present
Is connected to
How I perceive
Myself in my head.

I've Been

I've been living
In the expectation
Of tomorrow that I forgot to live today.

I Want To

I want
To become
The Monopoly
Of a specific craft.
The one who's
In a war
With his warcrafts.
I want to become
The alpha which hunts
And kills his prey
I want to quit
Being paralyzed
By these lines of sight
I want to quit
Being the Simba
Who runs from
Taking his rightful
Place as king
I want to stop
Living as the Patrick
Star who sleeps
Underneath the rock of greatness
I want to quit
Hiding myself
I want to. I want to.

Jack of All Trades

I played the Strings of a violin
Until I landed on puberty
I beat against the drums
Until the parts broke down
I moved around different States like
A Tasmanian Devil
The "Jack of all trades"
So many things I want
But not sure where to start
And how to start.

Open Up

Can I please open up the gift now?
It's been sitting around in the
Closet of my insanity
For to long now
When is my turn coming?

Close Out

In summary
There are more questions
Still not answered
There are no final conclusions
Just air breathing in and breathing out
So, closing this out with another
Blank chapter. Such is life, I guess.

Chapter 5: Auditions

Eighteen

The commencement has begun
So many different family support systems
In attendance for their babies'
First step into adulthood
Some friends will become strangers
While others stay together
For me, it's another one of those same old summers
Pack up the MTV crib house
And move back to a familiar area
There are people who I look
Forward to connecting with once again
Even a possible fling that got started
Out of nowhere on My Space for a year
Guess we will see what's going to happen
The destination might feel like home
I said "feel" because
Home still hasn't found me yet
And I know the underlying reasoning
I'm just not ready for grace
To help me deal with those demons
The next chapter is bittersweet in a sense
There are friends who I consider my brothers
We have each other's back
It's hard to say goodbye, but I've done it so many times
I'm used to leaving people behind.

Faces

Faces come and go
Some will stick around
Some will find other company
I'm just content to experience community.

Starting Over

Here we are
Back to square number one
In a church that opened my eyes
To some truth I didn't receive
Until I was 14
It's good to know I've been missed
By peers who haven't seen me for 5 years
It's almost like a big family reunion that's
Not going anywhere
Oh, "hey girl, it's finally nice to meet you"
You're quiet I see
That's cool with me
All of these pleasant memories
Is nostalgic to me
I never thought I would say this
But starting over here was a good thing.

Home Life

I would trap
Myself in the room
And never come out
When his presence
Was around
If I did come out,
Those positive vibes
In prayer times
As soon as I faced him
Were pulled from under me
And the only reaction I had
Was a loud pipe
That overrode each lecture.

Angry birds

The bird wanting to be free
Is trapped in a cage
Of rage
Once his lips try
Letting him out
There are fireworks of language
That flies across his direction
Leaving him more reasons
To hide himself in the cage.

Mono to Mono

Rather than go
Into the ring
I rather not
Deal with my issues.

Metro Bus

Oh, those good old
Rides where I could
Be alone with God
And learn a thing or two
About what I should
Be looking at now.

First Time for everything

Didn't expect those words
To be summoned upon your lips
Nothing ever was forced
And it's a little slip of the tongue
On your end of the line
Before the midnight hour settle in
I was caught off guard
But again, the conviction in your voice
Had me convinced it was genuine
It was my 1st time hearing this, and now
An unconditional love had played its cards
I drew out my King and she drew out her Queen
There were Diamonds of Hearts
Being expressed towards me
I just let it all happen naturally
Let's see where this goes next
I have to remember there will always
Be a first time for everything.

I Wanted

I wanted to give you sunshine
Because you were given rain
I wanted to give you happiness
Because you were going through pain
I wanted you to see a path towards light
When darkness was covering up your world
I wanted you to see the beauty of life
And these were the signs of why you wanted to be my girl.

Learner's Permit

I've had trouble being taught new tricks
Some are necessary
Some are questionable
In the end, I was able
To complete the challenges at hand.

On top

I stayed on top of due dates
Professor demands
And church activities.
But I wasn't on top
Of those little foxes
Living inside of me.

Youth to Young Adult

The news of a new chapter
Wasn't something that
Caught me off guard
It was long overdue
My stumbling block
Was not opening myself
Up for others to come in
And help me understand
The next steps.

Fading Away

What happened to the fire?
I could find wood in the woods
And rekindle the burning desires right away
Now all the flames go out 5 minutes after
I open my eyes
Where did I find the motivation to accept this new reality of fading away?

3-Week Absence

The beginning of this Fall
My absence had put me
Behind the eight ball
I was "damaged goods" to all
These sudden assumptions
About not seeing happiness again
The deep sorrow within kept
Me in a dark room downstairs
I wouldn't move for hours
As I sat and stared at 2K
For hours upon hours
My legs were locked to the ground
My head was lost in the crowd
And my spiritual appetite
Was being a servant to condemnation
This absence from reality had brought
A loneliness I had never seen
This shock had me confused by all
The sudden changes I saw around me
And with my identity in question
I didn't understand where I could
Go from here
Almost 21
No clarity here to pick me up
And give me a blueprint
I was searching. I was searching
I felt absent from the absence
I had no idea what I should do next.

Pushed

I'm being pushed down
Into the depths of a sea
Where I don't believe
I'll swim to shore
This time around
My thoughts are bombarded
By lack of masculine energy
As I lay here on my bed
I have no strength to get up
Grace seems occupied
Mercy appears to quit giving me second chances

Just push me into the depths of hell
I'm not worth fighting for anymore.

Costumes

I wore the nice black slacks
The white shirt
The black jacket
But then I went casual
You could tell the
Spark plug had been unplugged.

Volunteer

There I was in the pit
And Mercy said
"Look over here
There's a soul winner
Training going on this weekend
And I want you to volunteer"
Me? "Yes you"
Haven't you been watching
The past 3 months?
"Of course. That's why you need to go"
Okay, I guess
Where am I even going?
"Grab your friends and sister
It's time for a road trip"

I'll Never Forget

I'll never forget
Sitting in a backyard
With tears of joy
Flooding over 50 plus
Unqualified people
No suit and ties on
No religious protocols
They were genuine folks
Looking for a reason to be alive
Where the spirit
Flowed without anyone's interruption

Tanks were ready with water
And so was the same group
That experience had begun
To open my eyes and find
Hope once again.

Not Qualified

As we headed back home
From a weekend of spiritual bliss
I was looking for a blueprint
On how to rekindle the fire
My issue though
Was how can I start my own?
I'm not qualified enough I said
I'm not where I should be
I'm not even talking to God like I should be
Just look at the past year
Go find someone else who is probably
Better for the job than I am.

Chapter 6: Out of Tune

There I was

There I was
Standing between
My intention to become
And my intervention with sorrow.

Cycles

The rose was red
Then the rose was black
Seemed like the rose
Had lost her spark.
This cycle had me
Going back and forth.

Signs

The problems said stop
But I returned and said go
I was too afraid
Of having the first "Ex"
Stamped on my resume.

The Nice Guy

Hey, I'll be your friend
Hey, I'll keep those dreams to myself
Even though I would
Like to know you more
Even though I would
Like to find out if that reality is tangible
But that's fine
It's best not to focus on
What I really want
Put on those same old routines
There's nothing interesting going on here.

Hide and Seek

I hide myself
Behind these lines
While seeking for this
Spark of imagination
To rise inside.

Lost Soul

If I wrote a poem
For every moment
This soul has been lost
There wouldn't be any
Words that could end
With a period.

Edge

This Hulk Gamma
Rages on more and more
His encounters are still
Putting me on the edge
Of explosion.

Valentines Day

I think I should
Redefine this chapter
Of my life
As "break up day"
There wasn't any
Love being handed out
On this day
No, this day was full of
Tensions that were high as
Skyline Mountains
And our fumes were
Not interested in
Making peace with
Each other.

Last Minute Transition

The due date
For transcripts had arrived
Procrastination got a hold
Of me once again
My confidence was running low
Like a tank going on "E"
I didn't want to believe the in scripted
Word "Accepted" would manifest
In a returned email
Maybe it was the grades or maybe
I have projected the perception of rejection
Who knows the reason?
Thank God there were 2 hours left
To give myself a shot.

Here we go again

A week had gone by
Hopped on the bus
Headed back for home
Text messages coming from an old fling
Which should have remained dead
But I was already dead
Kissed and made up
Here we are back again
In hopes that our decision
To rekindle old flames.

Just Existing

I'm existing just to exist
Ask me how I'm doing?
My answer will be the same
I am good
Ask me how's work?
My answer will be
It's alright
The shifts are just enough
To give me another breath
I wrap myself in a dark room
Carrying so much weight
Doesn't seem I have a lot going
In a positive direction
So, for now I'll show up
Where I'm supposed to be
Sit in classes while zoning out
And just existing
That's all I see right now.

"Eeyore"

My countenance is low
My face has no emotions
I wish I could put myself
In the Hundred Acre Woods
Maybe then I could
Find a compelling reason
To become alive
And discover
The meaning of why
God created me.

Probably

The word probably
Has become the greatest
Enemy of my soul.
I just want to say the words yes or no
Without the sword of uncertainty
Piercing my desire for clarity.

Uninterested

It's crazy how I used
To care about leaving
A good impression
I would always wear the "Sunday best"
To feel good about myself
But now those impressions
Have drifted into the valley
Of depression
Throw on the light blue jeans
A red polo shirt
And go head to Sunday Morning Church
Where everyone else's morning doesn't
Have a song of mourning to wear on their shirt
Then go right back home
Head down the stairs
And sit in the man cave
As my eyes spend hours upon hours
Glued on a bunch of characters.
I justify my reasons for this way of thinking
And to be honest It's quite simple
There's no interest challenging
The comfort parts of my reality because
I've gotten the hang of this reality
I do not understand the value of trying new things
When those visions have already been impaired
I am just going to always rely
On survival tactics instead of
Ownership tactics.

Doomed

I started writing this paragraph in my head
Since I was 17
That I was colliding towards
A pit that would last forever
And here I am trying to pray
Yet it doesn't appear that
I'll ever see change.

A Sign

I opened the letter
And to my surprise
They accepted me
Despite the obvious
Calculations of my GPA.
Maybe this would become
The break I needed to start
Believing in myself again.

Shame

So, let's play another game of hide and go seek
How many times will I sit in the presence of guilt?
A voice cries out to let those urges go for good
Meanwhile I run back into her open arms
Even though conviction will catch up with me again.

Down the Drain

Stashed up all this cash
Only to watch the entire
Plan come crashing down
On this 91 Accord
Here I was making up assumptions
For my future
No way of going point A to B
No available funds because it was
All invested in this one accomplishment
Here I was feeling the weight of hopelessness
The stress was like a bad tune
It wasn't sounding good
All those expectations going down the drain
I thought to myself "so much for getting my one good break"
Now those breaks have turned into a problem I can't fix
And with only a month until the next phase of life begins
I couldn't believe the idea right now
Down the drain I went and didn't see a solution to help me out.

Change of Perspective

It was a rough spot
I didn't know where to turn
I had a mood of despair
Written all over my expressions
Started to regret not investigating
Before submitting to impulse
Despite all these different thoughts spinning around
I had this anchor of hope rising from the ashes
It came out of left field
It was the same exact aura
I experienced when the acceptance letter
Came across my desktop
Some how I mustered up the courage
To change the perspective
Impairing my ability to look
Beyond the current waves
And drown myself in a water of faith
Beyond anything I've gone through before.
I started knocking on doors that appeared
Out of reach
But this was a much-needed lesson.

Finding A Way

The compass was saying
Go East
Don't overthink just do like the
Slogan Nike would preach
It was a big task
However, you can't
Eat the whole Elephant in one bite
So, I took one bite at a time
And suddenly I found myself
Sitting in a classroom
With all the pieces
Being filled just in time
This is where my faith
Began to walk toward
The place of rest
There was still much to learn
But this was a good first step.

Lost

Everything that seems lost
Is going to be found.
Just glance at the skies
When the night arrives on scene
It appears hopeless
It appears all is lost
Then out of nowhere
The sun comes in like a flood
And everything that seemed lost
Was never lost.

My

My eyes are confused
My legs are broken
My lips are crushed
My soul is tired
My back is cracked
My lungs yearn
To connect with God's breath
My heart is angry
Yet it still has a seed of hope
And because of this
I won't be worried about
This new chapter I am in
I'll follow through
Until I find the peace
That puts together
Every missing piece
That's hindered me within.

Chapter 7: In Tune

First Day

Couldn't believe my own eyes
The colors were all different
The faces were all new
The ground I stood upon
Were full of vibrations
I'd never seen before
It was like opening day
In the NBA
It was a great milestone
After what appeared
Out of reach
Before I forget to leave this
Part out.
There was another 4-wheel vehicle
Waiting for me to pick up.
Christmas had come early for me.

Short Period

Never underestimate
How much you can
Elevate yourself
In a short period of time.

Fresh Motivation

The drive I had lost
Started kicking back
Into overdrive
This season gave me
Another reason to
Shake off those lies
Planted deep inside my mind
I said to myself this chapter
Is going to work out for my good
I've come too far to stop now.

Strong Start

I focused on kicking off
This semester like a kick returner
Opening up the game
With 6 points on the scoreboard.
No field goals were good enough.
I wanted to have long drives which
Didn't stall if I had to convert
On 3rd and longs
When studying time was demanded
I crawled up next to my desk in the bedroom
And tuned out every noise around me
This was a great feeling
Because I woke up having a task
With a compass pointing me
In a specific direction.

Not a Grade

Week 3 sitting in one of my favorite
Classes at the time
There was a moment where
A statement had punctured
My current beliefs about
High A's and High B's
She said, "the value
You hold within you
Is not a reflection of your grades
It doesn't matter how many
Perfect scores are given back
For your hard work
You are not your grade"
That quote followed me
Out the door
And travelled with me
Everywhere I went.

Failed

If you fail to pass
In finding your passion
You have already failed.

Mission Field

I remember having a flashback
Over one year ago
Going to what is called Youth Congress
I sat among 5000 plus students in a basketball stadium
A presentation was brought to the screen
Then a man would stand
before this large crowd
He spoke with passion about
The experience you would have on
This life changing trip
It was quite a speech that didn't go unheard
In his conclusion, he challenged us to
Stand up and make a commitment
Over to my right was my Youth Pastor
Who gazed toward our section
Daring us to follow his request
Even though I didn't see it ever happening
I was compelled enough to follow along
Now I'm seeing what hasn't been fulfilled
Since I am big on saying yes or saying no
That value was hung on my heart like a Christmas Candlelight
It was still Fall
But the seed had begun to grow.

Lola

One wild little girl
Always in high demand.
But those puppy eyes
Would steal my attention
From whatever I was doing.
All those long walks together
Helped me hit the reset button
When stress began sending
A wave of signals about
The context from every
Single text I had to interrupt
For upcoming exams
She would follow
Her own crowd
And that was herself
The only downside

Was she came into a house
As a rebound.

Loyalty

I'm looking around
For the hands that
Used to hold on
For dear life.
They've all withered away
Now I'm carrying the weights
Without the spotters
That stood over me
When I struggled to lift
Myself back up.

Not Subsiding

The voices still
Have the power
To erupt like a volcano
When him and I are
Standing in the same room
I want peace to
Subside the monsters
Which are inside me.
But my attitude
Won't allow me
To overcome the
Intense emotions
That remote controls me
The one I call father
Is just another human
To me right now.
When is this going to get better?

Long Distance

I still find her in my dreams
When I'm awake, you're the first one that comes to mind
Three years later and still going strong
Even though we're moons apart
The attraction is still consuming
Our hearts
The long weekend drive
Builds up the suspense.
Our stress fades away
When I show up
For those 48 hours
We just focus on
Maintaining the sparks
Which fly around like fireflies
Once I leave, we're back
To the missing stages
At least my life has taken
A good turn
And we might be
Seeing the horizon soon.

End of Semester

Yo, Jason, the exams
Have faded like the wind.
Our grades are looking
Attractive to our eyes.
Let's kick up our feet
Play with Lola
And binge watch Netflix
Until we fall asleep
We've earned our stripes
The "thick as thieves"
Celebration has started.

Man Cave

For hours upon hours
I laid my head
Across those fluffy delicate pillows.
No one heard my footsteps
Unless it was a scheduled
Appointment to work
A trip to the kitchen
Or showing up for church.
Morning and nights were pretty
Much me laying down with
Absolutely no kind of motivation
I stayed in the "Man Cave"
No one could bother me
And I didn't want to be bothered
My girl always found me unavailable
Because I had this motivation to finish
Watching "Lost"
This "Man Cave" exposed my true character
And that wasn't exactly what I had expected
After ending my semester on a high note.

On Campus

The moment finally happened
A feeling of independence
Had shown up on my radar
I had been yearning to get myself
Detached from my lack of ambitions
I thought a change of scenery
Would leave behind the
Character flaws inside of me
Five days per week being in the presence of Jay
What didn't get told to me was a chapter
Perseverance was preparing me for.

Honesty

After setting up the dorm
A long drive was next on the agenda
Two people having the space
To speak without distractions
Pushing down our vulnerable spots
I didn't expect myself
To open up this gaping hole
In my heart
Especially toward a woman
But some how I dug around
The roots and uprooted those wounds
By opening up about my father's absence
My tone would go down an octave
There were still chains
I was trying to break through
But honestly, I could
Have some room
This was stage one
But at least it's a start.

Branches

I still have branches
Of fury which press the
Buttons of my peace.

Chapter 8:   The Turning Point

Wake Up Call

There was a dream
Which followed me
Like a bunch of busy bodies
I can't recall the date nor time
But it was a constant reminder
Showing up all the time
The roller coaster picture
And flames of fire
Would press the repeat button
Over and over again
I knew God was trying
To wake me up from my slumber
There was a constant tug of war
Going on with my eternal destiny
Although the dehydration was still
Present in my spiritual connection
I still couldn't get that image out of my head
I wanted to find a magical eraser
But his grace wouldn't allow
This memory to fade out
It wouldn't leave me nor forsake me
The wake-up call was in full effect
There was no hiding in a "Man Cave"
It was coming in full force like the force
Of a Star Wars Jedi
And this is where chains
Would slowly bow down in submission.

Standing

The blissful weekend
Had come to fruition
Between our passions
For what we called Love
It started out pure, 4 years ago
It was something we both enjoyed
But as time moved forward
Those standards had been picked apart
Like a good apple going bad
Behind closed doors are secrets
I remember the voice of conviction screaming
In desperation in hopes I would
Make up my mind
An image had appeared on my screen
It was the boy who stood up
And made a commitment for what
Is called AYC
It wouldn't stop talking. It wouldn't leave me alone
Even if I could block the number
In my ear, that wouldn't be effective
After turning on the ignition
And pondering all this shame
There was a boldness which finally
Got a strong hold of me
For about 2 hours
I laid out what I allowed
And then I laid out the guidelines
That wouldn't be crossed anymore
The conversation was quite hard
But it needed to become a reality
The wake-up call had begun
Working on my shame.
And this was only the
Tip of this iceberg.

I Got To

I got to a point
Where I needed
The warmth of a hug
The devotions among other peers
The shaking of brotherly hands
The fellowship of like-minded folks
The accountability partners
Knowing about my whereabouts
The casket needed to rise
But I needed to borrow another shovel
To dig myself out of this pit
And it was up to me
To quit walking alone.

You Cannot

You cannot experience
Intimate connections
Until pride leaves
The room.

If you

If you have a face
That doesn't change its facial expressions
When all hell is breaking loose around you
That's a face worth getting to know
If you hold a hand
Which doesn't flinch
It's a hand worth holding on to
If you receive a checking in text
That's a good indicator
To respond and get even closer
But this happens
Only if you want to.

Spiritual Nourishment

For the first time
In over 2 years
I was getting fed
Some good meat
On a weekly basis
I found myself enjoying
This new season of spiritual release
I had yearned for, for a long time.
Now this nourishment
Had carried itself toward
A Shepherd I avoided because fear
Would keep whispering I'm not good enough
There I was though making a conscious
Effort in a high school auditorium
To get myself connected
It was a step in the right direction
I still had a long way to go.

Flamed Out

It had been almost 2 months
Since being in her presence
Both parties in high demand from the early
Semester demands
I saw our time apart as a test
I would either watch the flame stand tall
Or watch the flame fall into the waterfall of breakups
I made sure to give her attention
But whatever I did wasn't good enough
I began thinking back about the moment
It became one sided
Those 4 bus rides across different States
While giving up potential income and hang
Out with my little sibling
And those 5 voicemails left on the other line
To keep our love going because new
Boundaries were cutting the communication
From her outside world
The seasons where updates
Were being done through yahoo emails
That's when it hit me like a freight train
This isn't the love I deserve
This isn't all I'm worth
And this is where the flames
Started going cold.

Shepherd Introduction

I had a decision to make and
It was cutting me in two.
I swore an oath to never
Have one "Ex" stamped
On my resume
Well there I was in need of wisdom
It was Saturday evening
Where I took a leap
Of courage to connect
With someone who I only
Knew from the pulpit
Questions about career path
About the school I attended
Eased my nerves
Then he said
Is there anything else going on?
As soon as this happened
My confession had begun
I was lost and confused
I'll never forget the analogy
"God box", "career box", and "school box"
Focus on checking those 3 boxes
And you'll be able to save
Yourself any future troubles
I left in a state of ease
I followed with the call to action
And ended the romance forever
Haven't looked back since
Thank God for a Shepherd's Introduction.

Freedom

Free of late night calls
Free of confrontations
Free of voices going up different octaves
Free of being off the market
Free of wanting those desires
Free at last. Free at last

Movie Night

Movie night with my
Sister and her best friend
That was the original agenda
Until sickness dropped a sledgehammer
On my sibling's plan
I went anyways because she
Didn't want her friend to go alone
I went out because "Mr. Nice Guy"
Was my label
There wasn't any pressure
There weren't any intentions
Just two people out on a casual night
Enjoying the popcorn and flick
In the background, a plot was thickening
That would soon take an unexpected turn of events.

Let's Try Again

Loneliness had a segment
Prepped for me to watch
The moment my eyes fasted on the sun
And the moment my eyes drifted into a dream
Sudden buzzes were popping up
I figured a few exchanges wouldn't hurt
But that casual talk led to me
Open up again
I had to remind myself that I'm "on the market"
And I deserve a shot at love
Besides, there's an ocean of women
So, what do I have to lose?
Let's play again.

Moving Forward

Time has their act together
Always moving forward no matter
What is going on around them
If they never stop following their purpose
Of moving forward
Then why should we stop
If a new season is upon us?

Acceptance Letter

I opened the email
And what do you know
The promise I made
In front of those 5000 plus
Students had finally arrived
I didn't know what to expect
I didn't know what to even think
But a sense of purpose had started
Growing inside of me.

New Thing

I was pulled in like gravity
Our chemistry was less confusing
Than an H_2O formula
I thought to myself
This is exactly what
I've been looking for this whole time
Just a simple easy-going relationship
Disagreements? Yes
Conflicts? Yes
But quick to forgive
And quick to apologize
There was equal value
For maintaining the relationship
It was strange but great for me
This is exactly what I wanted.

Mission Field Answered

One week of spiritual encounters
With like minded Pentecostals
I felt out of place
But I was still embraced
When Monday came
A lot of decisions had
To be made.

Random Talent Show

Sitting in the back
My peers on the trip
Were expressing their gifts
I jotted some lines down
Then stood in front
And saw a gift
I never knew about
Until my lips
Began talking
It happened out of the blue
But there was a passion
That had me asking myself
Is this random or real?

Letting Go

I sent the message
Through a text message.
The message nobody likes to receive.
I was torn between serving
And staying with the second love
Who kept me stable
With all my unstable ways
She even dunked herself in water the right way
That's where a choice had to be made
And at times I wondered if grace
Had some more space to invade
The decision to head our separate ways
But as they say, life goes on
But I had to engage myself
With the passions I cared about
It was hard to say goodbye
It was hard to let go
I honestly wish it worked out
Right now, I need a break
To figure myself out
Hopefully the third time
Will be the lucky charm
Until then, I am hoping
For the best in both
Of our lives.

Now I see

There was a pencil
On my desk
A bunch of pages
Without ink smeared
In black
I started out
With different rhymes
Even got books
On how to write
My bones were shaking
But my hand would see
What actually would
Set my soul free.

Slow Burn

The next three
Months were a season
Of seeds getting watered.
The forms were filled out.
The approved message
That a campus ministry
Was going to happen
Would become a reality.
And the fire was laying
Down the passion that was lost
This time around I
Wouldn't allow the
Fresh burns to fizzle
Out anymore.

Unleashed

The leash was unleashed
I was a man possessed
With purpose
I was that Denzel, "Man on Fire" character
No brakes could
Stop my engine from moving.

Phone call

Hey Mom, what happened?
Well the family album
Is now collecting dust
Hope is absent
And will be absent forever.

Bed in Hell

The next 3 months
Had so many twists and turns
Nowhere to lay my head for rest
It was stress that couldn't be defined
My bed was laid out in hell
And I didn't see peace nowhere in sight.

One Picture

When the nightfall corrupted
My belief system
I reflected on a picture
With 50 kids surrounding
My brokenness in a different continent
Their smiles became my strength
Their acceptance became my joy
Their love became my weapon against fear
Their content state of mind became my source for gratitude
That one picture kept all hell inside of me from breaking loose.

First Confrontation

Face to face since the Spring
Outside in the brittle cold
Where my lips shivered in pride
But I had to face my inner demons
"Dad", I paused then proceeded to say
"I forgive you. I forgive you"
This anger needs to stop at this stop sign
His ears were open to receive
This was step one
But a good first step
The first honesty moment
I've had since the 14-year-old kid

Chapter 9: Debut

Found

I didn't find Poetry
Poetry found me.

My Lips

My lips can utter hope
My lips can utter doubt
My lips can utter love
My lips can utter fear
My lips can utter inspiration
My lips can utter discouragement
My lips can utter peace
My lips can utter burdens.

Forgiveness

The raging seas
Would come crashing down
At the sight of second chances
The current had a strong hold on me
But it wasn't enough to stop a cross
That reminded me I am messed up
I am just a person with a puzzle
Still being put together
So, bitterness you can exit stage right
I rather keep on rehearsing the line
"I forgive you", for the rest of my life.

Glass of Water

I'm going to pour
This glass of water
Into someone else's
Love cup that needs
To see what real love
Is really all about.
They might push me away
They might have trust issues
They might be uncommitted
They might drown in their fears
But no matter what happens
This glass of water
Is always going to pour
A love filled to the brim
Because it's not about
What you do for someone
It's about how you made them
Feel about you.

Won't Change

Love will always guide me
Love will always be the anchor of my soul
Love will always keep me whole
Love is who I am
And that won't ever change
No matter what storm comes next.

I AM

I am a writer
I am beautiful
I am great
I am powerful
I am inspiration
I am motivation
I am love
I am mercy
I am forgiving
I am passion
I am confidence
I am not a survivor but an overcomer
I am the best artists to ever stroke a pen
I am who God says I am.
And if the I AM had
Stated who He is with conviction
Then maybe it's time
I start viewing myself
The same way.

The Wind

I am no longer going to watch the wind pass me by
Where it travels, I will follow
East. West. North. South
It doesn't matter to me
I am not going to sit on
The sidelines anymore
When the door opens
I'm walking right in
Without second guessing myself
I will study the wind
Know it's every turn
Know it's every intention
When it moves, my faith moves
When it's still, my faith will be still
When it's bold, my faith will be bold
Whatever the wind plans to do today
I'll be ready for every season.

Perseverance

I have learned to keep
The book open
Until I understand
The lesson I need
To prosper when
The time is right.

Move the line

First and ten at the
ten-yard line
There is 90 yards
Of grass in front of me
I'm only focused on
Executing the playbook
And moving the process
Down toward the end zone
If a big play opens up
I'll take my chances
But the home-run play
Isn't the main objection
Let's move the line
So we can have
More victories at the
End of each process.

Old Self

The old version of me
Is now dead
I helped to bury him
With letters that keep
On plugging away.

Dear Jay: Part 2

What's going on Jay?
Congratulations on making it through
Your first life session about identity
You've been looking around
Like a Detective in search
Of evidence for quite a long time
It probably makes sense why
You found yourself watching
How masterminds work together
To piece together the facts in Criminal Minds
Remember I told you at 6 your folks
Would end up saying goodbye
And friends would disappear
Well it's a reality and a reality that'll take
Awhile to settle in
I know right now forgiveness is a sense of relief
But just know this is stage one of a 4 year
Healing process
Nothing ever changes overnight
Right now, the independence you're experiencing
Is quite a mountain to climb
You want establishment but instability
Is going to hang around for a little bit
You want a major break but from here on out
Every decision falls on your shoulders
There will be a major decision at some point
You'll make for yourself
And it will grow you up
To the man you see in yourself
For now, let the pen
Lay down on your heartbeat
Allow the creative impulse
To find its rhythm on every beat
There will be the same 14-year-old
Inner critic fighting you tooth and nail
You'll be tempted to pack up your treasures
And settle for leftovers
You'll even place this wonderful gift
In a crib for a period
But it won't succeed
You are now 23, with a lot of life to live
So, live it and watch the pieces
Become a masterpiece
Till next time Jay.

I always wanted

I always wanted
My imagination to run wild
Without limitations saying
"I can't think in those terms"
I always wanted
My dreams to have a sense
Of purpose and not the same
Old collect a paycheck
Every other week
I always wanted
A life where time
Isn't controlled by
A set schedule
I always wanted
More and that is
What I'm searching for now.

Chapter 10: Release Date

Puzzles

If you drop
A puzzle to the ground
It will no longer be together
Yes, my family album
Has missing pictures
But just like those pictures
I'll be able to piece my
Own together.

Anticipation

I stand at the doorway
Knowing the moment
Is going to arrive
I'll be ready because
I've been planning for this
Stage my whole life.

Drums, Keys, and Strings

Three instruments
Have made me see
Who I should be.

Walking Away

Even though he walked away
Locked the front door of his promises
And never came back
I picked up his tracks
And realized his path
Helped me reshape
The meaning of walking away.
When values didn't align with my beliefs
I used his blueprint for good.
I now see his decision
Helps protect my inner peace.
So, whoever doesn't value me
I can walk out holding my head high
I can allow the silence to handle my problems
I can let God fight the battles that have nothing to do with me.
What appeared as evil was meant for good
So, whenever I need to walk away, I will
Because I understand I am more than enough.

Change

Change has always been around
I changed in height
I changed in weight
I changed my tone of voice
I changed in puberty
I changed from 5th grade to 6th grade
I changed from one church to another church
I changed from MD to GA
I changed from GA to MD
I'm changing now from the
Family breakup
Change has always been constant
Change is coming no matter what
Change is making decisions
Without our consensus
I'm grateful for the gift of change
It's a blessing not a curse.

Adaptable

Whether I'm wearing a coat
Wearing a White-Polo Shirt
Wearing Nike Shorts
Wearing Denim Jeans
I can make the adjustments
In any season I face.

Hands

When Pilate had
Ordered the guards
To pierce Jesus' hands
There were holes nailed deeply between
His frail palms
In those palms were hands
That could understand the scars
People like us would have to carry
Scars in terms of not having a completed picture
Pictures such as not having
The father affirm his son when he's down and out
The mother caring for her children to kiss their wounds
The Thanksgiving and Christmas gatherings with family friends and strangers
The family circle having no circle of drawing closer together
The last names being different
Those hands are the hands I am after now
I know those hands better than a lot of people know
And yes, I get irritated with other pierced hands
Who witness their peers complain
About having their family around for too long
At least the support exists in the house
Our hands are still trying to figure those gaps out
We much rather have family problems stay in house
Than family problems which divide the house
But I want the hands with nails in your palms to know
Your holes aren't thorns in your flesh
Your holes are testimonies that should be expressed
Your holes are a reminder that you can feel the presence of death
And remain unshaken by what comes next.

Stand

I will stand even
If I have to stand
For what I believe
In by myself.

July 4th

July 4th happens
Everyday for me
I wake up deciding
What I should eat
What I should read
Who's in my circle
Who's not in my circle
When to spend time with God
What church to attend
What an amazing liberation
There is much to learn
And much to gain
The tribulation appeared
To knock me out
I prayed for space by myself
Earlier in the year
It didn't go as planned
But it's exactly what I always wanted
Freedom of choice
For a newborn man.

Remind Me

Dear God,
As I sit in this house
Of Strangers
Remind me that my current
Living space is going to get better
Remind me when stones hit my heart
Don't let it stop beating
Remind me when I doubt your existence
To show up when I am in that presence
Remind me to keep myself open
To the word impossibility
Remind me to take action
Without overthinking the consequences
Remind me of the good days ahead

When my soul feels the sting of death
Remind me to keep moving forward
When loneliness says you are by yourself
Remind me to pick myself back up
When life throws a curveball
Remind me to stand tall like the Rock
Who stood tall in his small town
Remind me to stop waiting
On the greatness that lives inside of me
Remind me to move the line
One day at a time
Remind me that You are a Father
Who wants me to manifest
The best version of me
Remind me that our connection
Hasn't died even if my emotions
Have another perspective
Remind me to play the game
Of truth and dare
Remind me to never apologize
For believing in the power of
Having a community of people
Building your faith up
Remind me not to be ashamed
To ask for someone's help
Remind me to always dream
For a life bigger than what
My eyes will ever see
Remind me to hope for the best
And to never bow down to the
Spirit of regret.

Chapter 11: Nominated

I've Gone

I've gotten this far
Let's see how much
Farther I can push myself.

Grace

If Grace had a name
Her name would be
Amazing.

House to House

I slept in four different
Houses during a one-year span
My lenses needed adjustments
On a month to month basis
Two basements and two rooms
Became my point of view
Even though it was a
Hard pill to digest
I got to experience
The feeling of being homeless
That is a feeling I wouldn't trade
In those pits, I found comfort
With the words I expressed
In the secret place about myself.

Respecter of Persons

If there was a time
When colors became
A desire to be around
It was located down south in two
Different churches 20 minutes apart
Same faces. Same groups. Same community
There weren't any open invitations
For black, blue, red, or orange
This disturbed my spirit
I only found cultural acceptance
In the school hallways
But the church hallways
Had cliques around me
I found Jesus more at my school
Than I did anywhere else in this season
Fast forward to 50 African kids in a picture
A Dashiki in my closet
A sister married to a Jamaican
Having more black cards
Than white cards in
My circle of influence
I enjoy beholding another
Eye color besides my own
Because it puts away the background checks
And embraces the presence of different colors.

Love Is

Love is who I am
It found me before I existed
Love doesn't scare me
Love doesn't run from me
Love is the greatest expression that mankind will ever see
The cross revealed that to me
Love might not find everyone I meet
But it's always going to follow me
It's going to remain open no matter what comes against me.

Hey Dad

Hey Dad,
You didn't give me the entire toolbox
I've had to care for myself
I've had to move on from myself
I've had to develop a walk with God by myself
I've had to find a career by myself
I've had to do a lot by myself
But there are tools I received before
All this chaos took place
Let's go back in time
The resistance started rising at 14
However, you were producing a healthy banana
Before the spoiled banana came to pass
The spoils I fixed myself because that wasn't your fault
Looking through your lenses of abandonment
It makes sense why you had trouble managing all this success
The pressure is serious when you carry all those burdens by yourself
You ask for help but you feel like no one can actually help
I'm not going to hold you hostage for the past you haven't laid to rest yet
Ever since I learned about Forgiveness
Blaming people for my problems is weak
It's not what I want to project
So, thank you for the lessons you could teach
Because I wouldn't be able to love others
With unconditional care had you not broken me.

Crowds

You go left
You go right
You stay in the middle
You wait
What about me?
You beat to your own drum.

Goliath

One day I am
To kill the "Goliath"
Inside of me
Then I'm going to
Resurrect the "Goliath"
That inspires me
To become a lion king
Who keeps his pride
In good standing.
And his flock ready
To slay their personal enemies.

Drive

Give me the wheel
I'll keep moving forward
Until the real Jay becomes real.

Chaos

I don't run from chaos
I thrive in chaos.

Poverty

In the depths of famine
I know my scarcity will
Disappear in the presence of abundance.

Grasshopper

Right now, I'm the little Grasshopper
I feel small
I feel unheard
There is one advantage
I am developing
And that is a
Leap of faith

Finish Line

I woke up
Smelled the roses
Breathed in the sun
Melted in my accomplishment
It was a Bachelor's Degree
But that day I got my
First Bachelor's
In Perseverance
In Grit
In Character
I have now reached the Finish Line.

What do I see?

What do I see?
There is anticipation on the horizon
A career path on the board
A new place of independence awaits
What do I see?
The pen has a lot to teach me
The English Language has much to learn
The Poet is still in development
What do I see?
Well I see a beginning to an end
A Genesis to a Revelation
A promise to a promise still being fulfilled
What do I see?
I see part one of myself
This is where I stop
I'm going to leave this final
Piece as a cliff hanger
That'll hang for awhile
What do I see?
To be continued…

www.ingramcontent.com/pod-product-compliance
Lightning Source LLC
Chambersburg PA
CBHW080416170426
43194CB00015B/2826